THE

BUSHCRAFT

101

FIELD LOG

Track and Record Your Wilderness Adventures

DAVE CANTERBURY

New York Times Bestselling Author

ADAMS MEDIA

NEW YORK LONDON TORONTO SYDNEY NEW DELHI

Adams Media
An Imprint of Simon & Schuster, LLC
100 Technology Center Drive
Stoughton, Massachusetts 02072

Copyright © 2024 by Simon & Schuster, LLC.

All rights reserved, including the right to reproduce this book or portions thereof in any form whatsoever. For information, address Adams Media Subsidiary Rights Department, 1230 Avenue of the Americas, New York, NY 10020.

First Adams Media trade paperback edition December 2024

ADAMS MEDIA and colophon are registered trademarks of Simon & Schuster, LLC.

Simon & Schuster: Celebrating 100 Years of Publishing in 2024

For information about special discounts for bulk purchases, please contact Simon & Schuster Special Sales at 1-866-506-1949 or business@simonandschuster.com.

The Simon & Schuster Speakers Bureau can bring authors to your live event. For more information or to book an event, contact the Simon & Schuster Speakers Bureau at 1-866-248-3049 or visit our website at www.simonspeakers.com.

Interior design by Sylvia McArdle
Interior images © Clipart.com; 123RF; Adobe Stock

Manufactured in China

10 9 8 7 6 5 4 3 2 1

ISBN 978-1-5072-2379-6

Many of the designations used by manufacturers and sellers to distinguish their products are claimed as trademarks. Where those designations appear in this book and Simon & Schuster, LLC, was aware of a trademark claim, the designations have been printed with initial capital letters.

Readers are urged to take all appropriate precautions before undertaking any how-to task. Always read and follow instructions and safety warnings for all tools and materials, and call in a professional if the task stretches your abilities too far. Although every effort has been made to provide the best possible information in this book, neither the publisher nor the author is responsible for accidents, injuries, or damage incurred as a result of tasks undertaken by readers. This book is not a substitute for professional services.

— Introduction —

Record your journey, step by step, with *The Bushcraft 101 Field Log*. From cataloging what you've packed and recording campsite specifics to making observations while out in the woods, you will find this notebook to be a useful tool in mastering the art of wilderness survival and exploration. The practical templates—along with open pages for general notes, findings, and impressions—give you direction and space to plan and capture the details of your trip.

Everything in your pack serves a purpose, and this notebook is no exception. It's a useful tool for outlining, navigating, and bettering your bushcraft skills. With this notebook, you'll be able to log each trip—or leg of your trip—so you feel prepared and observant while out in the woods. In addition, you'll have the opportunity to learn from what you've documented about your experiences to help inform your future outings. For example, you'll be able to see what you packed but didn't use, note how you built your shelter or started your fire, and more.

Practicing bushcraft is a great way to enjoy the outdoors. This field log gives you the space to record your experiences while also remaining safe and informed. Let this be the place where you both remember your successes and review the documented challenges you faced. Whether you're a novice or a seasoned bushcrafter, there is plenty to learn, and you can gain your most valuable lessons by going out and being in the wilderness.

As noted naturalist John Burroughs stated, "The pleasure and value of every walk or journey we take may be doubled to us by carefully noting down the impressions it makes upon us." Let this field log be the place where you learn from each journey you take.

4 | THE BUSHCRAFT 101 FIELD LOG

HOW TO USE THIS FIELD LOG

The field log is broken down into sections that each can be used for an entire trip, or for individual legs of a larger trip. Within the six pages of each section, you'll find space to record trip specifics, such as location, duration, and conditions; packing lists; navigation assistance; and observation fields—along with open space to write down any additional notes or information.

The prompts and lists are derived from my Bushcraft series of books. If you would like further information or additional resources, you can consult those titles for detailed instructions on how to build shelter, administer first aid, trap small game, and more.

The pocket at the back of this notebook is where you can store trail maps and writing implements.

TRIP SPECIFICS

This page of the field log contains information detailing the specifics of your trip, along with space to document the type of pack you're using and what's been packed.

Here you will want to record where and when you are going on your trek. This information will be important when cataloging your trip. It will also provide an important reference if you return to that particular location.

In addition to logging the location specifics, it's important to record the trip's duration, along with the weather and conditions of the trail. Each will impact your experiences and observations, as well as any future planning when returning to the location.

PACK LIST

You have many options when it comes to the pack you choose, the gear you pack, and the type of shelter you build.

Pack

Record the type of pack you decide to use. You have a number of different pack types to choose from, including a bed/blanket roll, rucksack, pack frame, and pack basket. Choose the pack that is most suitable for where you are going—and for what you need to bring with you.

Gear

This list is by no means exhaustive; however, it is a great reference tool to make sure you have the essential gear necessary on each journey. It is based on my 5 Cs of Survivability.

The 5 Cs are:

1. **Cutting tools** to manufacture needed items and process food.
2. **Combustion devices** for creating the fires needed not only to preserve and cook food but also to make medicines and provide needed warmth.
3. **Cover elements** to create a microclimate of protection from the elements.
4. **Containers** to carry water over distances or to protect collected food sources.
5. **Cordages** for bindings and lashings.

Within these five base elements are all the tools and knowledge you need to be prepared for emergencies. These items are the hardest to reproduce from natural material, take the largest amount of skill to reproduce, and control the conditions that most directly affect your body's core temperature.

In addition to listing what you decide to bring, you should also record what you ultimately used. If you didn't use it during your trip, leave it out next time. If you find you need it, you can add it again later.

CAMPSITE

SHELTER
- ☐ Tent
- ☐ Hammock and tarp
- ☐ Fly
- ☐ A-frame
- ☐ Lean-to
- ☐ Wedge
- ☐ OTHER: _____
- ☐ OTHER: _____

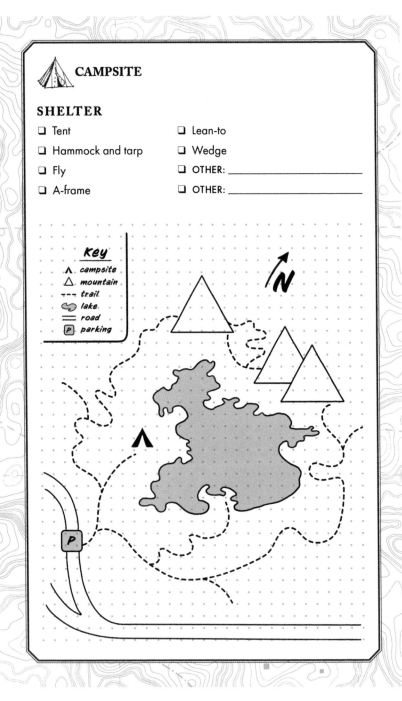

CAMPSITE MAP

This page details your campsite and gives you space to record its layout in relation to handrails, backstops, and baselines. In addition to noting the type of shelter you've constructed, you can record the location of water sources, trail heads, hilltops or ridgelines, along with any other landmarks to help with orientation. It's also useful to note the cardinal directions and create a key.

HOW TO USE THE PAUL (POSITIVE AZIMUTH UNIFORM LAYOUT) METHOD

Using the PAUL method will allow you to scout an unknown area and figure a straight line bearing back to camp without backtracking by reverse azimuths all the way. This can come in very handy if you've covered quite a bit of distance. To use this method, you will need to set up a log page in your journal for notes, and you will have to record bearings and distances to each point along the way. The easy way to accomplish this—and still get your scouting done—is to carry a flag or bandanna that is highly visible, preferably one that is orange.

Take an azimuth from your camp to a distant object. In your journal, record the azimuth and distance as you walk to the object. Once you are there, place your flag on the object and continue scouting around the area—but never lose sight of the flag. When you are ready to move on, go back to the flag and take another reading to a distant object. Walk to it, recording the bearing and paces again in your journal. Place the flag on the object and scout around.

Continue this procedure until you are ready to return to camp. Draw a map in your book on a small scale, using the points and distances you have recorded. Decide the scale based on any measuring device—for example, .25 inches = 100 meters. Once you have drawn the map, check your return azimuth from the last

8 | THE BUSHCRAFT 101 FIELD LOG

point to your camp and the distance. You could easily do this with sticks or rocks on the ground. You should then be able to travel back in a straight line.

OBSERVATIONS AND GENERAL FIELD NOTES

These four pages give you the space to record everything you've seen and done while in the wilderness. This information will provide helpful reference points for future trips, giving you the opportunity to record your observations of area flora and fauna, document the skills and techniques you've used, and learn what worked well—and what could be improved.

OBSERVATIONS

These fields are not exhaustive, but they do provide a starting point for your study of the environment around you. What type of wildlife have you seen—or seen evidence of? What type of plant life is in the area? You can take notes in the provided space and expand in the General Field Notes section to include sketches of tracks, descriptive details of plants and fungi, and more.

Remember: Do not ingest or use any foraged plants or fungi without properly identifying them.

CAMPSITE ACTIVITY

This is where you can document the purpose of your trip and whether or not it was achieved. You can note the wild game you trapped and what types of traps you used to ensnare each one. You can record your hunting or fishing, as well as the specific times and locations, so you have all that information for future use.

GENERAL FIELD NOTES

In addition to providing additional space for your observations and campsite activities, the General Field Notes provide room for you to record a number of other things, including notes on shelter-building and fire-starting. This will provide insight into what worked well, along with the ways in which you can improve your skills for next time.

You can also include important emergency contact information, document any first aid conducted on yourself or others in your party, and keep track of important supplies such as food rations.

The General Field Notes section can also be used to aid in navigation. You can keep track of your pace, record your azimuths, and note any additional details that will help with self-mapping and orientation.

LOCATION:

DATE:

COORDINATES: _____ ELEVATION: _____

TERRAIN: _____

WEATHER:

TEMPERATURE: _____ CONDITIONS: _____

DURATION

- ❑ Loop
- ❑ Out and back
- ❑ Day trip
- ❑ Overnight
- ❑ Extended stay
- ❑ OTHER: _____

PACK

TYPE: _____

GEAR

	Used (Y/N)		Used (Y/N)
❑ Compass		❑ Blanket	
❑ Cord		❑ Axe	
❑ Cup		❑ Rope	
❑ Lighter		❑ Water bottle	
❑ Stakes		❑	
❑ Pot		❑	
❑ Tarp		❑	
❑ Knife		❑	
❑ Skillet		❑	

# CAMPSITE

SHELTER
- ❏ Tent
- ❏ Hammock and tarp
- ❏ Fly
- ❏ A-frame
- ❏ Lean-to
- ❏ Wedge
- ❏ OTHER: _____
- ❏ OTHER: _____

OBSERVATIONS

WILDLIFE:

TREES AND OTHER FLORA:

RIVERS, LAKES, OTHER WATER:

CAMPSITE ACTIVITY

BUILDS:

TRAPPED:

HUNTED/FISHED:

GENERAL FIELD NOTES

GENERAL FIELD NOTES

GENERAL FIELD NOTES

LOCATION:

DATE:

COORDINATES: _____ ELEVATION: _____

TERRAIN: _____

WEATHER:

TEMPERATURE: _____ CONDITIONS: _____

DURATION

- ❏ Loop
- ❏ Out and back
- ❏ Day trip
- ❏ Overnight
- ❏ Extended stay
- ❏ OTHER: _____

PACK

TYPE: _____

GEAR

	Used (Y/N)		Used (Y/N)
❏ Compass		❏ Blanket	
❏ Cord		❏ Axe	
❏ Cup		❏ Rope	
❏ Lighter		❏ Water bottle	
❏ Stakes		❏	
❏ Pot		❏	
❏ Tarp		❏	
❏ Knife		❏	
❏ Skillet		❏	

CAMPSITE

SHELTER

- ❏ Tent
- ❏ Hammock and tarp
- ❏ Fly
- ❏ A-frame
- ❏ Lean-to
- ❏ Wedge
- ❏ OTHER: _____
- ❏ OTHER: _____

OBSERVATIONS

WILDLIFE:

TREES AND OTHER FLORA:

RIVERS, LAKES, OTHER WATER:

CAMPSITE ACTIVITY

BUILDS:

TRAPPED:

HUNTED/FISHED:

GENERAL FIELD NOTES

GENERAL FIELD NOTES

GENERAL FIELD NOTES

LOCATION:

DATE:

COORDINATES: _____ ELEVATION: _____

TERRAIN: _____

WEATHER:

TEMPERATURE: _____ CONDITIONS: _____

DURATION

- ❏ Loop
- ❏ Out and back
- ❏ Day trip
- ❏ Overnight
- ❏ Extended stay
- ❏ OTHER: _____

PACK

TYPE: _____

GEAR

	Used (Y/N)		Used (Y/N)
❏ Compass		❏ Blanket	
❏ Cord		❏ Axe	
❏ Cup		❏ Rope	
❏ Lighter		❏ Water bottle	
❏ Stakes		❏	
❏ Pot		❏	
❏ Tarp		❏	
❏ Knife		❏	
❏ Skillet		❏	

CAMPSITE

SHELTER

- ❏ Tent
- ❏ Hammock and tarp
- ❏ Fly
- ❏ A-frame
- ❏ Lean-to
- ❏ Wedge
- ❏ OTHER: _____
- ❏ OTHER: _____

OBSERVATIONS

WILDLIFE:

_____

_____

_____

TREES AND OTHER FLORA:

_____

_____

_____

RIVERS, LAKES, OTHER WATER:

_____

_____

_____

CAMPSITE ACTIVITY

BUILDS:

_____

_____

_____

TRAPPED:

_____

_____

_____

HUNTED/FISHED:

_____

_____

_____

GENERAL FIELD NOTES

GENERAL FIELD NOTES

GENERAL FIELD NOTES

LOCATION:

DATE:

COORDINATES: _____ ELEVATION: _____

TERRAIN: _____

WEATHER: ☀ 🌤 ⛅ ☁ 🌦 🌧 🌦 ⛈ 🌨

TEMPERATURE: _____ CONDITIONS: _____

DURATION

❑ Loop   ❑ Overnight

❑ Out and back   ❑ Extended stay

❑ Day trip   ❑ OTHER: _____

PACK

TYPE: _____

GEAR

	Used (Y/N)		Used (Y/N)
❑ Compass		❑ Blanket	
❑ Cord		❑ Axe	
❑ Cup		❑ Rope	
❑ Lighter		❑ Water bottle	
❑ Stakes		❑	
❑ Pot		❑	
❑ Tarp		❑	
❑ Knife		❑	
❑ Skillet		❑	

 **CAMPSITE**

SHELTER
- ☐ Tent
- ☐ Hammock and tarp
- ☐ Fly
- ☐ A-frame
- ☐ Lean-to
- ☐ Wedge
- ☐ OTHER: _____
- ☐ OTHER: _____

OBSERVATIONS

WILDLIFE:

TREES AND OTHER FLORA:

RIVERS, LAKES, OTHER WATER:

CAMPSITE ACTIVITY

BUILDS:

TRAPPED:

HUNTED/FISHED:

GENERAL FIELD NOTES

GENERAL FIELD NOTES

GENERAL FIELD NOTES

LOCATION:

DATE:

COORDINATES: _____ ELEVATION: _____

TERRAIN: _____

WEATHER:

TEMPERATURE: _____ CONDITIONS: _____

DURATION

- ❑ Loop
- ❑ Out and back
- ❑ Day trip
- ❑ Overnight
- ❑ Extended stay
- ❑ OTHER: _____

PACK

TYPE: _____

GEAR

	Used (Y/N)		Used (Y/N)
❑ Compass		❑ Blanket	
❑ Cord		❑ Axe	
❑ Cup		❑ Rope	
❑ Lighter		❑ Water bottle	
❑ Stakes		❑	
❑ Pot		❑	
❑ Tarp		❑	
❑ Knife		❑	
❑ Skillet		❑	

 **CAMPSITE**

SHELTER

- ❏ Tent
- ❏ Hammock and tarp
- ❏ Fly
- ❏ A-frame
- ❏ Lean-to
- ❏ Wedge
- ❏ OTHER: _____
- ❏ OTHER: _____

OBSERVATIONS

WILDLIFE:

_____
_____
_____

TREES AND OTHER FLORA:

_____
_____
_____

RIVERS, LAKES, OTHER WATER:

_____
_____
_____

CAMPSITE ACTIVITY

BUILDS:

_____
_____
_____

TRAPPED:

_____
_____
_____

HUNTED/FISHED:

_____
_____
_____

GENERAL FIELD NOTES

GENERAL FIELD NOTES

GENERAL FIELD NOTES

LOCATION:

DATE:

COORDINATES: _____ ELEVATION: _____

TERRAIN: _____

WEATHER:

TEMPERATURE: _____ CONDITIONS: _____

DURATION

- ❑ Loop
- ❑ Out and back
- ❑ Day trip
- ❑ Overnight
- ❑ Extended stay
- ❑ OTHER: _____

PACK

TYPE: _____

GEAR

	Used (Y/N)		Used (Y/N)
❑ Compass		❑ Blanket	
❑ Cord		❑ Axe	
❑ Cup		❑ Rope	
❑ Lighter		❑ Water bottle	
❑ Stakes		❑	
❑ Pot		❑	
❑ Tarp		❑	
❑ Knife		❑	
❑ Skillet		❑	

 **CAMPSITE**

SHELTER

- ❏ Tent
- ❏ Hammock and tarp
- ❏ Fly
- ❏ A-frame
- ❏ Lean-to
- ❏ Wedge
- ❏ OTHER: _____
- ❏ OTHER: _____

OBSERVATIONS

WILDLIFE:
_____
_____
_____

TREES AND OTHER FLORA:
_____
_____
_____

RIVERS, LAKES, OTHER WATER:
_____
_____
_____

CAMPSITE ACTIVITY

BUILDS:
_____
_____
_____

TRAPPED:
_____
_____
_____

HUNTED/FISHED:
_____
_____
_____

GENERAL FIELD NOTES

GENERAL FIELD NOTES

LOCATION:

DATE:

COORDINATES: _____ ELEVATION: _____

TERRAIN: _____

WEATHER:

TEMPERATURE: _____ CONDITIONS: _____

DURATION

- ❑ Loop
- ❑ Out and back
- ❑ Day trip
- ❑ Overnight
- ❑ Extended stay
- ❑ OTHER: _____

PACK

TYPE: _____

GEAR

	Used (Y/N)		Used (Y/N)
❑ Compass		❑ Blanket	
❑ Cord		❑ Axe	
❑ Cup		❑ Rope	
❑ Lighter		❑ Water bottle	
❑ Stakes		❑	
❑ Pot		❑	
❑ Tarp		❑	
❑ Knife		❑	
❑ Skillet		❑	

 **CAMPSITE**

SHELTER

- ❏ Tent
- ❏ Hammock and tarp
- ❏ Fly
- ❏ A-frame
- ❏ Lean-to
- ❏ Wedge
- ❏ OTHER: _____
- ❏ OTHER: _____

OBSERVATIONS

WILDLIFE:
___
___
___

TREES AND OTHER FLORA:
___
___
___

RIVERS, LAKES, OTHER WATER:
___
___
___

CAMPSITE ACTIVITY

BUILDS:
___
___
___

TRAPPED:
___
___
___

HUNTED/FISHED:
___
___
___

GENERAL FIELD NOTES

GENERAL FIELD NOTES

GENERAL FIELD NOTES

LOCATION:

DATE:

COORDINATES: _____ ELEVATION: _____

TERRAIN: _____

WEATHER: ☀ 🌤 ⛅ ☁ 🌦 🌧 🌧 ⛈ 🌨

TEMPERATURE: _____ CONDITIONS: _____

DURATION

- ❑ Loop
- ❑ Out and back
- ❑ Day trip
- ❑ Overnight
- ❑ Extended stay
- ❑ OTHER: _____

PACK

TYPE: _____

GEAR

	Used (Y/N)		Used (Y/N)
❑ Compass		❑ Blanket	
❑ Cord		❑ Axe	
❑ Cup		❑ Rope	
❑ Lighter		❑ Water bottle	
❑ Stakes		❑	
❑ Pot		❑	
❑ Tarp		❑	
❑ Knife		❑	
❑ Skillet		❑	

 **CAMPSITE**

SHELTER

- ❏ Tent
- ❏ Hammock and tarp
- ❏ Fly
- ❏ A-frame
- ❏ Lean-to
- ❏ Wedge
- ❏ OTHER: _____
- ❏ OTHER: _____

👓 OBSERVATIONS

WILDLIFE:

_____

_____

_____

TREES AND OTHER FLORA:

_____

_____

_____

RIVERS, LAKES, OTHER WATER:

_____

_____

_____

🔥 CAMPSITE ACTIVITY

BUILDS:

_____

_____

_____

TRAPPED:

_____

_____

_____

HUNTED/FISHED:

_____

_____

_____

GENERAL FIELD NOTES

GENERAL FIELD NOTES

GENERAL FIELD NOTES

LOCATION:

DATE:

COORDINATES: _____ ELEVATION: _____

TERRAIN: _____

WEATHER: ☀ 🌤 ⛅ 🌥 🌦 🌧 🌧 ⛈ 🌨

TEMPERATURE: _____ CONDITIONS: _____

DURATION

❑ Loop ❑ Overnight

❑ Out and back ❑ Extended stay

❑ Day trip ❑ OTHER: _____

PACK

TYPE: _____

GEAR

	Used (Y/N)		Used (Y/N)
❑ Compass		❑ Blanket	
❑ Cord		❑ Axe	
❑ Cup		❑ Rope	
❑ Lighter		❑ Water bottle	
❑ Stakes		❑	
❑ Pot		❑	
❑ Tarp		❑	
❑ Knife		❑	
❑ Skillet		❑	

CAMPSITE

SHELTER

- ❏ Tent
- ❏ Hammock and tarp
- ❏ Fly
- ❏ A-frame
- ❏ Lean-to
- ❏ Wedge
- ❏ OTHER: _____
- ❏ OTHER: _____

👓 OBSERVATIONS

WILDLIFE:
_____
_____
_____

TREES AND OTHER FLORA:
_____
_____
_____

RIVERS, LAKES, OTHER WATER:
_____
_____
_____

🔥 CAMPSITE ACTIVITY

BUILDS:
_____
_____
_____

TRAPPED:
_____
_____
_____

HUNTED/FISHED:
_____
_____
_____

GENERAL FIELD NOTES

GENERAL FIELD NOTES

GENERAL FIELD NOTES

LOCATION:

DATE:

COORDINATES: _____ ELEVATION: _____

TERRAIN: _____

WEATHER:

TEMPERATURE: _____ CONDITIONS: _____

DURATION

- ❑ Loop
- ❑ Out and back
- ❑ Day trip
- ❑ Overnight
- ❑ Extended stay
- ❑ OTHER: _____

PACK

TYPE: _____

GEAR

	Used (Y/N)		Used (Y/N)
❑ Compass		❑ Blanket	
❑ Cord		❑ Axe	
❑ Cup		❑ Rope	
❑ Lighter		❑ Water bottle	
❑ Stakes		❑	
❑ Pot		❑	
❑ Tarp		❑	
❑ Knife		❑	
❑ Skillet		❑	

 **CAMPSITE**

SHELTER

- ❏ Tent
- ❏ Hammock and tarp
- ❏ Fly
- ❏ A-frame
- ❏ Lean-to
- ❏ Wedge
- ❏ OTHER: _____
- ❏ OTHER: _____

👓 OBSERVATIONS

WILDLIFE:

_____

_____

_____

TREES AND OTHER FLORA:

_____

_____

_____

RIVERS, LAKES, OTHER WATER:

_____

_____

_____

🔥 CAMPSITE ACTIVITY

BUILDS:

_____

_____

_____

TRAPPED:

_____

_____

_____

HUNTED/FISHED:

_____

_____

_____

GENERAL FIELD NOTES

GENERAL FIELD NOTES

GENERAL FIELD NOTES

LOCATION:

DATE:

COORDINATES: _____ ELEVATION: _____

TERRAIN: _____

WEATHER: ☀ ⛅ 🌤 ☁ 🌦 🌧 🌧 ⛈ 🌨

TEMPERATURE: _____ CONDITIONS: _____

DURATION

- ❑ Loop
- ❑ Out and back
- ❑ Day trip
- ❑ Overnight
- ❑ Extended stay
- ❑ OTHER: _____

PACK

TYPE: _____

GEAR

	Used (Y/N)		Used (Y/N)
❑ Compass		❑ Blanket	
❑ Cord		❑ Axe	
❑ Cup		❑ Rope	
❑ Lighter		❑ Water bottle	
❑ Stakes		❑	
❑ Pot		❑	
❑ Tarp		❑	
❑ Knife		❑	
❑ Skillet		❑	

 **CAMPSITE**

SHELTER

- ❏ Tent
- ❏ Hammock and tarp
- ❏ Fly
- ❏ A-frame
- ❏ Lean-to
- ❏ Wedge
- ❏ OTHER: _____
- ❏ OTHER: _____

OBSERVATIONS

WILDLIFE:
___
___
___

TREES AND OTHER FLORA:
___
___
___

RIVERS, LAKES, OTHER WATER:
___
___
___

CAMPSITE ACTIVITY

BUILDS:
___
___
___

TRAPPED:
___
___
___

HUNTED/FISHED:
___
___
___

GENERAL FIELD NOTES

GENERAL FIELD NOTES

GENERAL FIELD NOTES

LOCATION:

DATE:

COORDINATES: _____ ELEVATION: _____

TERRAIN: _____

WEATHER:

TEMPERATURE: _____ CONDITIONS: _____

DURATION

❑ Loop ❑ Overnight

❑ Out and back ❑ Extended stay

❑ Day trip ❑ OTHER: _____

PACK

TYPE: _____

GEAR

	Used (Y/N)		Used (Y/N)
❑ Compass		❑ Blanket	
❑ Cord		❑ Axe	
❑ Cup		❑ Rope	
❑ Lighter		❑ Water bottle	
❑ Stakes		❑	
❑ Pot		❑	
❑ Tarp		❑	
❑ Knife		❑	
❑ Skillet		❑	

 **CAMPSITE**

SHELTER

- ❏ Tent
- ❏ Hammock and tarp
- ❏ Fly
- ❏ A-frame
- ❏ Lean-to
- ❏ Wedge
- ❏ OTHER: _____
- ❏ OTHER: _____

OBSERVATIONS

WILDLIFE:

_____
_____
_____
_____

TREES AND OTHER FLORA:

_____
_____
_____
_____

RIVERS, LAKES, OTHER WATER:

_____
_____
_____
_____

CAMPSITE ACTIVITY

BUILDS:

_____
_____
_____
_____

TRAPPED:

_____
_____
_____
_____

HUNTED/FISHED:

_____
_____
_____
_____

GENERAL FIELD NOTES

GENERAL FIELD NOTES

GENERAL FIELD NOTES

LOCATION:

DATE:

COORDINATES: _____ ELEVATION: _____

TERRAIN: _____

WEATHER:

TEMPERATURE: _____ CONDITIONS: _____

DURATION

- ❏ Loop
- ❏ Out and back
- ❏ Day trip
- ❏ Overnight
- ❏ Extended stay
- ❏ OTHER: _____

PACK

TYPE: _____

GEAR

	Used (Y/N)		Used (Y/N)
❏ Compass		❏ Blanket	
❏ Cord		❏ Axe	
❏ Cup		❏ Rope	
❏ Lighter		❏ Water bottle	
❏ Stakes		❏	
❏ Pot		❏	
❏ Tarp		❏	
❏ Knife		❏	
❏ Skillet		❏	

 **CAMPSITE**

SHELTER

- ❏ Tent
- ❏ Hammock and tarp
- ❏ Fly
- ❏ A-frame
- ❏ Lean-to
- ❏ Wedge
- ❏ OTHER: _____
- ❏ OTHER: _____

OBSERVATIONS

WILDLIFE:
_____
_____
_____

TREES AND OTHER FLORA:
_____
_____
_____

RIVERS, LAKES, OTHER WATER:
_____
_____
_____

CAMPSITE ACTIVITY

BUILDS:
_____
_____
_____

TRAPPED:
_____
_____
_____

HUNTED/FISHED:
_____
_____
_____

GENERAL FIELD NOTES

GENERAL FIELD NOTES

GENERAL FIELD NOTES

LOCATION:

DATE:

COORDINATES: _____ ELEVATION: _____

TERRAIN: _____

WEATHER:

TEMPERATURE: _____ CONDITIONS: _____

DURATION

- ❑ Loop
- ❑ Out and back
- ❑ Day trip
- ❑ Overnight
- ❑ Extended stay
- ❑ OTHER: _____

PACK

TYPE: _____

GEAR

	Used (Y/N)		Used (Y/N)
❑ Compass		❑ Blanket	
❑ Cord		❑ Axe	
❑ Cup		❑ Rope	
❑ Lighter		❑ Water bottle	
❑ Stakes		❑	
❑ Pot		❑	
❑ Tarp		❑	
❑ Knife		❑	
❑ Skillet		❑	

 **CAMPSITE**

SHELTER

- ❏ Tent
- ❏ Hammock and tarp
- ❏ Fly
- ❏ A-frame
- ❏ Lean-to
- ❏ Wedge
- ❏ OTHER: _____
- ❏ OTHER: _____

👓 OBSERVATIONS

WILDLIFE:
___
___
___

TREES AND OTHER FLORA:
___
___
___

RIVERS, LAKES, OTHER WATER:
___
___
___

🔥 CAMPSITE ACTIVITY

BUILDS:
___
___
___

TRAPPED:
___
___
___

HUNTED/FISHED:
___
___
___

GENERAL FIELD NOTES

GENERAL FIELD NOTES

GENERAL FIELD NOTES

LOCATION:

DATE:

COORDINATES: _____ ELEVATION: _____

TERRAIN: _____

WEATHER: ☀ 🌤 ⛅ 🌥 🌦 🌧 🌧 ⛈ 🌨

TEMPERATURE: _____ CONDITIONS: _____

DURATION

❑ Loop
❑ Out and back
❑ Day trip

❑ Overnight
❑ Extended stay
❑ OTHER: _____

PACK

TYPE: _____

GEAR

	Used (Y/N)		Used (Y/N)
❑ Compass		❑ Blanket	
❑ Cord		❑ Axe	
❑ Cup		❑ Rope	
❑ Lighter		❑ Water bottle	
❑ Stakes		❑	
❑ Pot		❑	
❑ Tarp		❑	
❑ Knife		❑	
❑ Skillet		❑	

 **CAMPSITE**

SHELTER

- ❏ Tent
- ❏ Hammock and tarp
- ❏ Fly
- ❏ A-frame
- ❏ Lean-to
- ❏ Wedge
- ❏ OTHER: _____
- ❏ OTHER: _____

OBSERVATIONS

WILDLIFE:
_____
_____
_____

TREES AND OTHER FLORA:
_____
_____
_____

RIVERS, LAKES, OTHER WATER:
_____
_____
_____

CAMPSITE ACTIVITY

BUILDS:
_____
_____
_____

TRAPPED:
_____
_____
_____

HUNTED/FISHED:
_____
_____
_____

GENERAL FIELD NOTES

GENERAL FIELD NOTES

GENERAL FIELD NOTES

LOCATION:

DATE:

COORDINATES: _____ ELEVATION: _____

TERRAIN: _____

WEATHER:

TEMPERATURE: _____ CONDITIONS: _____

DURATION

- ❑ Loop
- ❑ Out and back
- ❑ Day trip
- ❑ Overnight
- ❑ Extended stay
- ❑ OTHER: _____

PACK
TYPE: _____

GEAR

	Used (Y/N)		Used (Y/N)
❑ Compass		❑ Blanket	
❑ Cord		❑ Axe	
❑ Cup		❑ Rope	
❑ Lighter		❑ Water bottle	
❑ Stakes		❑	
❑ Pot		❑	
❑ Tarp		❑	
❑ Knife		❑	
❑ Skillet		❑	

CAMPSITE

SHELTER

- ❏ Tent
- ❏ Hammock and tarp
- ❏ Fly
- ❏ A-frame
- ❏ Lean-to
- ❏ Wedge
- ❏ OTHER: _____
- ❏ OTHER: _____

OBSERVATIONS

WILDLIFE:
_____
_____
_____

TREES AND OTHER FLORA:
_____
_____
_____

RIVERS, LAKES, OTHER WATER:
_____
_____
_____

CAMPSITE ACTIVITY

BUILDS:
_____
_____
_____

TRAPPED:
_____
_____
_____

HUNTED/FISHED:
_____
_____
_____

GENERAL FIELD NOTES

GENERAL FIELD NOTES

GENERAL FIELD NOTES

LOCATION:

DATE:

COORDINATES: _____ ELEVATION: _____

TERRAIN: _____

WEATHER:

TEMPERATURE: _____ CONDITIONS: _____

DURATION

- ❑ Loop
- ❑ Out and back
- ❑ Day trip
- ❑ Overnight
- ❑ Extended stay
- ❑ OTHER: _____

PACK

TYPE: _____

GEAR

	Used (Y/N)		Used (Y/N)
❑ Compass		❑ Blanket	
❑ Cord		❑ Axe	
❑ Cup		❑ Rope	
❑ Lighter		❑ Water bottle	
❑ Stakes		❑	
❑ Pot		❑	
❑ Tarp		❑	
❑ Knife		❑	
❑ Skillet		❑	

CAMPSITE

SHELTER
- ❏ Tent
- ❏ Hammock and tarp
- ❏ Fly
- ❏ A-frame
- ❏ Lean-to
- ❏ Wedge
- ❏ OTHER: _____
- ❏ OTHER: _____

👁 OBSERVATIONS

WILDLIFE:
___
___
___

TREES AND OTHER FLORA:
___
___
___

RIVERS, LAKES, OTHER WATER:
___
___
___

🔥 CAMPSITE ACTIVITY

BUILDS:
___
___
___

TRAPPED:
___
___
___

HUNTED/FISHED:
___
___
___

GENERAL FIELD NOTES

GENERAL FIELD NOTES

GENERAL FIELD NOTES

LOCATION:

DATE:

COORDINATES: _____ ELEVATION: _____

TERRAIN: _____

WEATHER: ☀ 🌤 ⛅ ☁ 🌦 🌧 🌧 ⛈ 🌨

TEMPERATURE: _____ CONDITIONS: _____

DURATION

- ❑ Loop
- ❑ Out and back
- ❑ Day trip
- ❑ Overnight
- ❑ Extended stay
- ❑ OTHER: _____

PACK
TYPE: _____

GEAR

	Used (Y/N)		Used (Y/N)
❑ Compass		❑ Blanket	
❑ Cord		❑ Axe	
❑ Cup		❑ Rope	
❑ Lighter		❑ Water bottle	
❑ Stakes		❑	
❑ Pot		❑	
❑ Tarp		❑	
❑ Knife		❑	
❑ Skillet		❑	

 **CAMPSITE**

SHELTER

- ❏ Tent
- ❏ Hammock and tarp
- ❏ Fly
- ❏ A-frame
- ❏ Lean-to
- ❏ Wedge
- ❏ OTHER: _____
- ❏ OTHER: _____

OBSERVATIONS

WILDLIFE:
_____
_____
_____

TREES AND OTHER FLORA:
_____
_____
_____

RIVERS, LAKES, OTHER WATER:
_____
_____
_____

CAMPSITE ACTIVITY

BUILDS:
_____
_____
_____

TRAPPED:
_____
_____
_____

HUNTED/FISHED:
_____
_____
_____

GENERAL FIELD NOTES

GENERAL FIELD NOTES

GENERAL FIELD NOTES

LOCATION:

DATE:

COORDINATES: _____ ELEVATION: _____

TERRAIN: _____

WEATHER:

TEMPERATURE: _____ CONDITIONS: _____

DURATION

- ☐ Loop
- ☐ Out and back
- ☐ Day trip
- ☐ Overnight
- ☐ Extended stay
- ☐ OTHER: _____

PACK

TYPE: _____

GEAR

	Used (Y/N)		Used (Y/N)
☐ Compass		☐ Blanket	
☐ Cord		☐ Axe	
☐ Cup		☐ Rope	
☐ Lighter		☐ Water bottle	
☐ Stakes		☐	
☐ Pot		☐	
☐ Tarp		☐	
☐ Knife		☐	
☐ Skillet		☐	

CAMPSITE

SHELTER
- ❏ Tent
- ❏ Hammock and tarp
- ❏ Fly
- ❏ A-frame
- ❏ Lean-to
- ❏ Wedge
- ❏ OTHER: _____
- ❏ OTHER: _____

OBSERVATIONS

WILDLIFE:

TREES AND OTHER FLORA:

RIVERS, LAKES, OTHER WATER:

CAMPSITE ACTIVITY

BUILDS:

TRAPPED:

HUNTED/FISHED:

GENERAL FIELD NOTES

GENERAL FIELD NOTES

GENERAL FIELD NOTES

LOCATION:

DATE:

COORDINATES: _____ ELEVATION: _____

TERRAIN: _____

WEATHER:

TEMPERATURE: _____ CONDITIONS: _____

DURATION

- ❑ Loop
- ❑ Out and back
- ❑ Day trip
- ❑ Overnight
- ❑ Extended stay
- ❑ OTHER: _____

PACK

TYPE: _____

GEAR

	Used (Y/N)		Used (Y/N)
❑ Compass		❑ Blanket	
❑ Cord		❑ Axe	
❑ Cup		❑ Rope	
❑ Lighter		❑ Water bottle	
❑ Stakes		❑	
❑ Pot		❑	
❑ Tarp		❑	
❑ Knife		❑	
❑ Skillet		❑	

 **CAMPSITE**

SHELTER

- ❏ Tent
- ❏ Hammock and tarp
- ❏ Fly
- ❏ A-frame
- ❏ Lean-to
- ❏ Wedge
- ❏ OTHER: _____
- ❏ OTHER: _____

OBSERVATIONS

WILDLIFE:

TREES AND OTHER FLORA:

RIVERS, LAKES, OTHER WATER:

CAMPSITE ACTIVITY

BUILDS:

TRAPPED:

HUNTED/FISHED:

GENERAL FIELD NOTES

GENERAL FIELD NOTES

GENERAL FIELD NOTES

LOCATION:

DATE:

COORDINATES: _____ ELEVATION: _____

TERRAIN: _____

WEATHER: ☀ 🌤 ⛅ ☁ 🌦 🌧 🌧 ⛈ 🌨

TEMPERATURE: _____ CONDITIONS: _____

DURATION

- ❑ Loop
- ❑ Out and back
- ❑ Day trip
- ❑ Overnight
- ❑ Extended stay
- ❑ OTHER: _____

PACK

TYPE: _____

GEAR

	Used (Y/N)		Used (Y/N)
❑ Compass		❑ Blanket	
❑ Cord		❑ Axe	
❑ Cup		❑ Rope	
❑ Lighter		❑ Water bottle	
❑ Stakes		❑	
❑ Pot		❑	
❑ Tarp		❑	
❑ Knife		❑	
❑ Skillet		❑	

# CAMPSITE

SHELTER

- ❏ Tent
- ❏ Hammock and tarp
- ❏ Fly
- ❏ A-frame
- ❏ Lean-to
- ❏ Wedge
- ❏ OTHER: _____
- ❏ OTHER: _____

👓 OBSERVATIONS

WILDLIFE:
___

TREES AND OTHER FLORA:
___

RIVERS, LAKES, OTHER WATER:
___

🔥 CAMPSITE ACTIVITY

BUILDS:
___

TRAPPED:
___

HUNTED/FISHED:
___

GENERAL FIELD NOTES

GENERAL FIELD NOTES

GENERAL FIELD NOTES

LOCATION:

DATE:

COORDINATES: _____ ELEVATION: _____

TERRAIN: _____

WEATHER: ☀ 🌤 ⛅ ☁ 🌦 🌧 🌧 ⛈ 🌨

TEMPERATURE: _____ CONDITIONS: _____

DURATION

- ❏ Loop
- ❏ Out and back
- ❏ Day trip
- ❏ Overnight
- ❏ Extended stay
- ❏ OTHER: _____

PACK

TYPE: _____

GEAR

	Used (Y/N)		Used (Y/N)
❏ Compass		❏ Blanket	
❏ Cord		❏ Axe	
❏ Cup		❏ Rope	
❏ Lighter		❏ Water bottle	
❏ Stakes		❏	
❏ Pot		❏	
❏ Tarp		❏	
❏ Knife		❏	
❏ Skillet		❏	

CAMPSITE

SHELTER

- ❏ Tent
- ❏ Hammock and tarp
- ❏ Fly
- ❏ A-frame
- ❏ Lean-to
- ❏ Wedge
- ❏ OTHER: _____
- ❏ OTHER: _____

OBSERVATIONS

WILDLIFE:

_____
_____
_____
_____

TREES AND OTHER FLORA:

_____
_____
_____
_____

RIVERS, LAKES, OTHER WATER:

_____
_____
_____
_____

CAMPSITE ACTIVITY

BUILDS:

_____
_____
_____
_____

TRAPPED:

_____
_____
_____
_____

HUNTED/FISHED:

_____
_____
_____
_____

GENERAL FIELD NOTES

GENERAL FIELD NOTES

GENERAL FIELD NOTES

LOCATION:

DATE:

COORDINATES: _____ ELEVATION: _____

TERRAIN: _____

WEATHER:

TEMPERATURE: _____ CONDITIONS: _____

DURATION

- ❏ Loop
- ❏ Out and back
- ❏ Day trip
- ❏ Overnight
- ❏ Extended stay
- ❏ OTHER: _____

PACK

TYPE: _____

GEAR

	Used (Y/N)		Used (Y/N)
❏ Compass		❏ Blanket	
❏ Cord		❏ Axe	
❏ Cup		❏ Rope	
❏ Lighter		❏ Water bottle	
❏ Stakes		❏	
❏ Pot		❏	
❏ Tarp		❏	
❏ Knife		❏	
❏ Skillet		❏	

CAMPSITE

SHELTER

- ❑ Tent
- ❑ Hammock and tarp
- ❑ Fly
- ❑ A-frame
- ❑ Lean-to
- ❑ Wedge
- ❑ OTHER: _____
- ❑ OTHER: _____

OBSERVATIONS

WILDLIFE:

_____

_____

_____

TREES AND OTHER FLORA:

_____

_____

_____

RIVERS, LAKES, OTHER WATER:

_____

_____

_____

CAMPSITE ACTIVITY

BUILDS:

_____

_____

_____

TRAPPED:

_____

_____

_____

HUNTED/FISHED:

_____

_____

_____

GENERAL FIELD NOTES

GENERAL FIELD NOTES

GENERAL FIELD NOTES

LOCATION:

DATE:

COORDINATES: _____ ELEVATION: _____

TERRAIN: _____

WEATHER:

TEMPERATURE: _____ CONDITIONS: _____

DURATION

- ❑ Loop
- ❑ Out and back
- ❑ Day trip
- ❑ Overnight
- ❑ Extended stay
- ❑ OTHER: _____

PACK

TYPE: _____

GEAR

	Used (Y/N)		Used (Y/N)
❑ Compass		❑ Blanket	
❑ Cord		❑ Axe	
❑ Cup		❑ Rope	
❑ Lighter		❑ Water bottle	
❑ Stakes		❑	
❑ Pot		❑	
❑ Tarp		❑	
❑ Knife		❑	
❑ Skillet		❑	

 **CAMPSITE**

SHELTER

- ❏ Tent
- ❏ Hammock and tarp
- ❏ Fly
- ❏ A-frame
- ❏ Lean-to
- ❏ Wedge
- ❏ OTHER: _____
- ❏ OTHER: _____

OBSERVATIONS

WILDLIFE:
___

TREES AND OTHER FLORA:
___

RIVERS, LAKES, OTHER WATER:
___

CAMPSITE ACTIVITY

BUILDS:
___

TRAPPED:
___

HUNTED/FISHED:
___

GENERAL FIELD NOTES

GENERAL FIELD NOTES

GENERAL FIELD NOTES

LOCATION:

DATE:

COORDINATES: _____ ELEVATION: _____

TERRAIN: _____

WEATHER: ☀ 🌤 ⛅ ☁ 🌦 🌧 🌧 ⛈ 🌨

TEMPERATURE: _____ CONDITIONS: _____

DURATION

- ❑ Loop
- ❑ Out and back
- ❑ Day trip
- ❑ Overnight
- ❑ Extended stay
- ❑ OTHER: _____

PACK

TYPE: _____

GEAR

	Used (Y/N)		Used (Y/N)
❑ Compass		❑ Blanket	
❑ Cord		❑ Axe	
❑ Cup		❑ Rope	
❑ Lighter		❑ Water bottle	
❑ Stakes		❑	
❑ Pot		❑	
❑ Tarp		❑	
❑ Knife		❑	
❑ Skillet		❑	

 **CAMPSITE**

SHELTER

- ❏ Tent
- ❏ Hammock and tarp
- ❏ Fly
- ❏ A-frame
- ❏ Lean-to
- ❏ Wedge
- ❏ OTHER: _____
- ❏ OTHER: _____

OBSERVATIONS

WILDLIFE:
___
___
___

TREES AND OTHER FLORA:
___
___
___

RIVERS, LAKES, OTHER WATER:
___
___
___

CAMPSITE ACTIVITY

BUILDS:
___
___
___

TRAPPED:
___
___
___

HUNTED/FISHED:
___
___
___

GENERAL FIELD NOTES

GENERAL FIELD NOTES

GENERAL FIELD NOTES

LOCATION:

DATE:

COORDINATES: _____ ELEVATION: _____

TERRAIN: _____

WEATHER: ☀ ⛅ 🌤 ☁ 🌦 🌧 🌧 ⛈ 🌨

TEMPERATURE: _____ CONDITIONS: _____

DURATION

❑ Loop
❑ Out and back
❑ Day trip

❑ Overnight
❑ Extended stay
❑ OTHER: _____

PACK

TYPE: _____

GEAR

	Used (Y/N)		Used (Y/N)
❑ Compass		❑ Blanket	
❑ Cord		❑ Axe	
❑ Cup		❑ Rope	
❑ Lighter		❑ Water bottle	
❑ Stakes		❑	
❑ Pot		❑	
❑ Tarp		❑	
❑ Knife		❑	
❑ Skillet		❑	

CAMPSITE

SHELTER

- ❏ Tent
- ❏ Hammock and tarp
- ❏ Fly
- ❏ A-frame
- ❏ Lean-to
- ❏ Wedge
- ❏ OTHER: _____
- ❏ OTHER: _____

OBSERVATIONS

WILDLIFE:

TREES AND OTHER FLORA:

RIVERS, LAKES, OTHER WATER:

CAMPSITE ACTIVITY

BUILDS:

TRAPPED:

HUNTED/FISHED:

GENERAL FIELD NOTES

GENERAL FIELD NOTES

GENERAL FIELD NOTES

LOCATION:

DATE:

COORDINATES: _____ ELEVATION: _____

TERRAIN: _____

WEATHER: ☀ ⛅ ☁ ☁ 🌦 ☁ 🌧 ⛈ 🌨

TEMPERATURE: _____ CONDITIONS: _____

DURATION

- ❑ Loop
- ❑ Out and back
- ❑ Day trip
- ❑ Overnight
- ❑ Extended stay
- ❑ OTHER: _____

PACK

TYPE: _____

GEAR

	Used (Y/N)		Used (Y/N)
❑ Compass		❑ Blanket	
❑ Cord		❑ Axe	
❑ Cup		❑ Rope	
❑ Lighter		❑ Water bottle	
❑ Stakes		❑	
❑ Pot		❑	
❑ Tarp		❑	
❑ Knife		❑	
❑ Skillet		❑	

 **CAMPSITE**

SHELTER

- ❏ Tent
- ❏ Hammock and tarp
- ❏ Fly
- ❏ A-frame
- ❏ Lean-to
- ❏ Wedge
- ❏ OTHER: _____
- ❏ OTHER: _____

OBSERVATIONS

WILDLIFE:
___
___
___

TREES AND OTHER FLORA:
___
___
___

RIVERS, LAKES, OTHER WATER:
___
___
___

CAMPSITE ACTIVITY

BUILDS:
___
___
___

TRAPPED:
___
___
___

HUNTED/FISHED:
___
___
___

GENERAL FIELD NOTES

GENERAL FIELD NOTES

GENERAL FIELD NOTES

LOCATION:

DATE:

COORDINATES: _____ ELEVATION: _____

TERRAIN: _____

WEATHER:

TEMPERATURE: _____ CONDITIONS: _____

DURATION

- ❑ Loop
- ❑ Out and back
- ❑ Day trip
- ❑ Overnight
- ❑ Extended stay
- ❑ OTHER: _____

PACK

TYPE: _____

GEAR

	Used (Y/N)		Used (Y/N)
❑ Compass		❑ Blanket	
❑ Cord		❑ Axe	
❑ Cup		❑ Rope	
❑ Lighter		❑ Water bottle	
❑ Stakes		❑	
❑ Pot		❑	
❑ Tarp		❑	
❑ Knife		❑	
❑ Skillet		❑	

CAMPSITE

SHELTER

- ☐ Tent
- ☐ Hammock and tarp
- ☐ Fly
- ☐ A-frame
- ☐ Lean-to
- ☐ Wedge
- ☐ OTHER: _____
- ☐ OTHER: _____

👁 OBSERVATIONS

WILDLIFE:
_____
_____
_____

TREES AND OTHER FLORA:
_____
_____
_____

RIVERS, LAKES, OTHER WATER:
_____
_____
_____

🔥 CAMPSITE ACTIVITY

BUILDS:
_____
_____
_____

TRAPPED:
_____
_____
_____

HUNTED/FISHED:
_____
_____
_____

GENERAL FIELD NOTES

GENERAL FIELD NOTES

GENERAL FIELD NOTES

LOCATION:

DATE:

COORDINATES: _____ ELEVATION: _____

TERRAIN: _____

WEATHER:

TEMPERATURE: _____ CONDITIONS: _____

DURATION

- ❏ Loop
- ❏ Out and back
- ❏ Day trip
- ❏ Overnight
- ❏ Extended stay
- ❏ OTHER: _____

PACK

TYPE: _____

GEAR

	Used (Y/N)		Used (Y/N)
❏ Compass		❏ Blanket	
❏ Cord		❏ Axe	
❏ Cup		❏ Rope	
❏ Lighter		❏ Water bottle	
❏ Stakes		❏	
❏ Pot		❏	
❏ Tarp		❏	
❏ Knife		❏	
❏ Skillet		❏	

CAMPSITE

SHELTER

- ☐ Tent
- ☐ Hammock and tarp
- ☐ Fly
- ☐ A-frame
- ☐ Lean-to
- ☐ Wedge
- ☐ OTHER: _____
- ☐ OTHER: _____

OBSERVATIONS

WILDLIFE:

TREES AND OTHER FLORA:

RIVERS, LAKES, OTHER WATER:

CAMPSITE ACTIVITY

BUILDS:

TRAPPED:

HUNTED/FISHED:

GENERAL FIELD NOTES

GENERAL FIELD NOTES

GENERAL FIELD NOTES

LOCATION:

DATE:

COORDINATES: _____ ELEVATION: _____

TERRAIN: _____

WEATHER:

TEMPERATURE: _____ CONDITIONS: _____

DURATION

- ❑ Loop
- ❑ Out and back
- ❑ Day trip
- ❑ Overnight
- ❑ Extended stay
- ❑ OTHER: _____

PACK

TYPE: _____

GEAR

	Used (Y/N)		Used (Y/N)
❑ Compass		❑ Blanket	
❑ Cord		❑ Axe	
❑ Cup		❑ Rope	
❑ Lighter		❑ Water bottle	
❑ Stakes		❑	
❑ Pot		❑	
❑ Tarp		❑	
❑ Knife		❑	
❑ Skillet		❑	

 **CAMPSITE**

SHELTER

- ❏ Tent
- ❏ Hammock and tarp
- ❏ Fly
- ❏ A-frame
- ❏ Lean-to
- ❏ Wedge
- ❏ OTHER: _____
- ❏ OTHER: _____

OBSERVATIONS

WILDLIFE:
_____
_____
_____

TREES AND OTHER FLORA:
_____
_____
_____

RIVERS, LAKES, OTHER WATER:
_____
_____
_____

CAMPSITE ACTIVITY

BUILDS:
_____
_____
_____

TRAPPED:
_____
_____
_____

HUNTED/FISHED:
_____
_____
_____

GENERAL FIELD NOTES

GENERAL FIELD NOTES

GENERAL FIELD NOTES

LOCATION:

DATE:

COORDINATES: _____ ELEVATION: _____

TERRAIN: _____

WEATHER: ☀ 🌤 ⛅ ☁ 🌦 🌧 🌧 ⛈ 🌨

TEMPERATURE: _____ CONDITIONS: _____

DURATION

- ❏ Loop
- ❏ Out and back
- ❏ Day trip
- ❏ Overnight
- ❏ Extended stay
- ❏ OTHER: _____

PACK

TYPE: _____

GEAR

	Used (Y/N)		Used (Y/N)
❏ Compass		❏ Blanket	
❏ Cord		❏ Axe	
❏ Cup		❏ Rope	
❏ Lighter		❏ Water bottle	
❏ Stakes		❏	
❏ Pot		❏	
❏ Tarp		❏	
❏ Knife		❏	
❏ Skillet		❏	

 **CAMPSITE**

SHELTER

- ❏ Tent
- ❏ Hammock and tarp
- ❏ Fly
- ❏ A-frame
- ❏ Lean-to
- ❏ Wedge
- ❏ OTHER: _____
- ❏ OTHER: _____

OBSERVATIONS

WILDLIFE:
___

TREES AND OTHER FLORA:
___

RIVERS, LAKES, OTHER WATER:
___

CAMPSITE ACTIVITY

BUILDS:
___

TRAPPED:
___

HUNTED/FISHED:
___

GENERAL FIELD NOTES

GENERAL FIELD NOTES

GENERAL FIELD NOTES

LOCATION:

DATE:

COORDINATES: _____ ELEVATION: _____

TERRAIN: _____

WEATHER: ☀ 🌤 ⛅ ☁ 🌦 🌧 🌧 ⛈ 🌨

TEMPERATURE: _____ CONDITIONS: _____

DURATION

❑ Loop
❑ Out and back
❑ Day trip

❑ Overnight
❑ Extended stay
❑ OTHER: _____

PACK

TYPE: _____

GEAR

	Used (Y/N)		Used (Y/N)
❑ Compass		❑ Blanket	
❑ Cord		❑ Axe	
❑ Cup		❑ Rope	
❑ Lighter		❑ Water bottle	
❑ Stakes		❑	
❑ Pot		❑	
❑ Tarp		❑	
❑ Knife		❑	
❑ Skillet		❑	

 **CAMPSITE**

SHELTER

- ❏ Tent
- ❏ Hammock and tarp
- ❏ Fly
- ❏ A-frame
- ❏ Lean-to
- ❏ Wedge
- ❏ OTHER: _____
- ❏ OTHER: _____

OBSERVATIONS

WILDLIFE:

TREES AND OTHER FLORA:

RIVERS, LAKES, OTHER WATER:

CAMPSITE ACTIVITY

BUILDS:

TRAPPED:

HUNTED/FISHED:

GENERAL FIELD NOTES

GENERAL FIELD NOTES

GENERAL FIELD NOTES

LOCATION:

DATE:

COORDINATES: _____ ELEVATION: _____

TERRAIN: _____

WEATHER: ☀ 🌤 ⛅ ☁ 🌦 🌧 🌧 ⛈ 🌨

TEMPERATURE: _____ CONDITIONS: _____

DURATION

❏ Loop
❏ Out and back
❏ Day trip
❏ Overnight
❏ Extended stay
❏ OTHER: _____

PACK
TYPE: _____

GEAR

	Used (Y/N)		Used (Y/N)
❏ Compass		❏ Blanket	
❏ Cord		❏ Axe	
❏ Cup		❏ Rope	
❏ Lighter		❏ Water bottle	
❏ Stakes		❏	
❏ Pot		❏	
❏ Tarp		❏	
❏ Knife		❏	
❏ Skillet		❏	

CAMPSITE

SHELTER

- ❏ Tent
- ❏ Hammock and tarp
- ❏ Fly
- ❏ A-frame
- ❏ Lean-to
- ❏ Wedge
- ❏ OTHER: _____
- ❏ OTHER: _____

OBSERVATIONS

WILDLIFE:
___
___
___

TREES AND OTHER FLORA:
___
___
___

RIVERS, LAKES, OTHER WATER:
___
___
___

CAMPSITE ACTIVITY

BUILDS:
___
___
___

TRAPPED:
___
___
___

HUNTED/FISHED:
___
___
___

GENERAL FIELD NOTES

GENERAL FIELD NOTES

GENERAL FIELD NOTES

LOCATION:

DATE:

COORDINATES: _____ ELEVATION: _____

TERRAIN: _____

WEATHER:

TEMPERATURE: _____ CONDITIONS: _____

DURATION

- ❑ Loop
- ❑ Out and back
- ❑ Day trip
- ❑ Overnight
- ❑ Extended stay
- ❑ OTHER: _____

PACK

TYPE: _____

GEAR

	Used (Y/N)		Used (Y/N)
❑ Compass		❑ Blanket	
❑ Cord		❑ Axe	
❑ Cup		❑ Rope	
❑ Lighter		❑ Water bottle	
❑ Stakes		❑	
❑ Pot		❑	
❑ Tarp		❑	
❑ Knife		❑	
❑ Skillet		❑	

 **CAMPSITE**

SHELTER

- ❏ Tent
- ❏ Hammock and tarp
- ❏ Fly
- ❏ A-frame
- ❏ Lean-to
- ❏ Wedge
- ❏ OTHER: _____
- ❏ OTHER: _____

OBSERVATIONS

WILDLIFE:
_____
_____
_____

TREES AND OTHER FLORA:
_____
_____
_____

RIVERS, LAKES, OTHER WATER:
_____
_____
_____

CAMPSITE ACTIVITY

BUILDS:
_____
_____
_____

TRAPPED:
_____
_____
_____

HUNTED/FISHED:
_____
_____
_____

GENERAL FIELD NOTES

GENERAL FIELD NOTES

GENERAL FIELD NOTES

LOCATION:

DATE:

COORDINATES: _____ ELEVATION: _____

TERRAIN: _____

WEATHER:

TEMPERATURE: _____ CONDITIONS: _____

DURATION

❑ Loop ❑ Overnight

❑ Out and back ❑ Extended stay

❑ Day trip ❑ OTHER: _____

PACK

TYPE: _____

GEAR

	Used (Y/N)		Used (Y/N)
❑ Compass		❑ Blanket	
❑ Cord		❑ Axe	
❑ Cup		❑ Rope	
❑ Lighter		❑ Water bottle	
❑ Stakes		❑	
❑ Pot		❑	
❑ Tarp		❑	
❑ Knife		❑	
❑ Skillet		❑	

CAMPSITE

SHELTER

- ❏ Tent
- ❏ Hammock and tarp
- ❏ Fly
- ❏ A-frame
- ❏ Lean-to
- ❏ Wedge
- ❏ OTHER: _____
- ❏ OTHER: _____

OBSERVATIONS

WILDLIFE:

TREES AND OTHER FLORA:

RIVERS, LAKES, OTHER WATER:

CAMPSITE ACTIVITY

BUILDS:

TRAPPED:

HUNTED/FISHED:

GENERAL FIELD NOTES

GENERAL FIELD NOTES

GENERAL FIELD NOTES

LOCATION:

DATE:

COORDINATES: _____ ELEVATION: _____

TERRAIN: _____

WEATHER: ☀ ⛅ ☁ ☁ 🌦 ☁ 🌧 ⛈ 🌨

TEMPERATURE: _____ CONDITIONS: _____

DURATION

- ❏ Loop
- ❏ Out and back
- ❏ Day trip
- ❏ Overnight
- ❏ Extended stay
- ❏ OTHER: _____

PACK
TYPE: _____

GEAR

	Used (Y/N)		Used (Y/N)
❏ Compass		❏ Blanket	
❏ Cord		❏ Axe	
❏ Cup		❏ Rope	
❏ Lighter		❏ Water bottle	
❏ Stakes		❏	
❏ Pot		❏	
❏ Tarp		❏	
❏ Knife		❏	
❏ Skillet		❏	

 **CAMPSITE**

SHELTER

- ❏ Tent
- ❏ Hammock and tarp
- ❏ Fly
- ❏ A-frame
- ❏ Lean-to
- ❏ Wedge
- ❏ OTHER: _____
- ❏ OTHER: _____

OBSERVATIONS

WILDLIFE:
_____
_____
_____

TREES AND OTHER FLORA:
_____
_____
_____

RIVERS, LAKES, OTHER WATER:
_____
_____
_____

CAMPSITE ACTIVITY

BUILDS:
_____
_____
_____

TRAPPED:
_____
_____
_____

HUNTED/FISHED:
_____
_____
_____

GENERAL FIELD NOTES

GENERAL FIELD NOTES

GENERAL FIELD NOTES

LOCATION:

DATE:

COORDINATES: _____ ELEVATION: _____

TERRAIN: _____

WEATHER:

TEMPERATURE: _____ CONDITIONS: _____

DURATION

- ❑ Loop
- ❑ Out and back
- ❑ Day trip
- ❑ Overnight
- ❑ Extended stay
- ❑ OTHER: _____

PACK

TYPE: _____

GEAR

	Used (Y/N)		Used (Y/N)
❑ Compass		❑ Blanket	
❑ Cord		❑ Axe	
❑ Cup		❑ Rope	
❑ Lighter		❑ Water bottle	
❑ Stakes		❑	
❑ Pot		❑	
❑ Tarp		❑	
❑ Knife		❑	
❑ Skillet		❑	

CAMPSITE

SHELTER

- ❏ Tent
- ❏ Hammock and tarp
- ❏ Fly
- ❏ A-frame
- ❏ Lean-to
- ❏ Wedge
- ❏ OTHER: _____
- ❏ OTHER: _____

👓 OBSERVATIONS

WILDLIFE:
_____
_____
_____

TREES AND OTHER FLORA:
_____
_____
_____

RIVERS, LAKES, OTHER WATER:
_____
_____
_____

🔥 CAMPSITE ACTIVITY

BUILDS:
_____
_____
_____

TRAPPED:
_____
_____
_____

HUNTED/FISHED:
_____
_____
_____

GENERAL FIELD NOTES

GENERAL FIELD NOTES

GENERAL FIELD NOTES

LOCATION:

DATE:

COORDINATES: _____ ELEVATION: _____

TERRAIN: _____

WEATHER:

TEMPERATURE: _____ CONDITIONS: _____

DURATION

- ❑ Loop
- ❑ Out and back
- ❑ Day trip
- ❑ Overnight
- ❑ Extended stay
- ❑ OTHER: _____

PACK
TYPE: _____

GEAR

	Used (Y/N)		Used (Y/N)
❑ Compass		❑ Blanket	
❑ Cord		❑ Axe	
❑ Cup		❑ Rope	
❑ Lighter		❑ Water bottle	
❑ Stakes		❑	
❑ Pot		❑	
❑ Tarp		❑	
❑ Knife		❑	
❑ Skillet		❑	

 **CAMPSITE**

SHELTER

- ☐ Tent
- ☐ Hammock and tarp
- ☐ Fly
- ☐ A-frame
- ☐ Lean-to
- ☐ Wedge
- ☐ OTHER: _____
- ☐ OTHER: _____

OBSERVATIONS

WILDLIFE:

_____
_____
_____

TREES AND OTHER FLORA:

_____
_____
_____

RIVERS, LAKES, OTHER WATER:

_____
_____
_____

CAMPSITE ACTIVITY

BUILDS:

_____
_____
_____

TRAPPED:

_____
_____
_____

HUNTED/FISHED:

_____
_____
_____

GENERAL FIELD NOTES

GENERAL FIELD NOTES

GENERAL FIELD NOTES

LOCATION:

DATE:

COORDINATES: _____ ELEVATION: _____

TERRAIN: _____

WEATHER:

TEMPERATURE: _____ CONDITIONS: _____

DURATION

- ❑ Loop
- ❑ Out and back
- ❑ Day trip
- ❑ Overnight
- ❑ Extended stay
- ❑ OTHER: _____

PACK

TYPE: _____

GEAR

	Used (Y/N)		Used (Y/N)
❑ Compass		❑ Blanket	
❑ Cord		❑ Axe	
❑ Cup		❑ Rope	
❑ Lighter		❑ Water bottle	
❑ Stakes		❑	
❑ Pot		❑	
❑ Tarp		❑	
❑ Knife		❑	
❑ Skillet		❑	

 **CAMPSITE**

SHELTER

- ❏ Tent
- ❏ Hammock and tarp
- ❏ Fly
- ❏ A-frame
- ❏ Lean-to
- ❏ Wedge
- ❏ OTHER: _____
- ❏ OTHER: _____

OBSERVATIONS

WILDLIFE:

TREES AND OTHER FLORA:

RIVERS, LAKES, OTHER WATER:

CAMPSITE ACTIVITY

BUILDS:

TRAPPED:

HUNTED/FISHED:

GENERAL FIELD NOTES

GENERAL FIELD NOTES

GENERAL FIELD NOTES

LOCATION:

DATE:

COORDINATES: _____ ELEVATION: _____

TERRAIN: _____

WEATHER:

TEMPERATURE: _____ CONDITIONS: _____

DURATION

- ❑ Loop
- ❑ Out and back
- ❑ Day trip
- ❑ Overnight
- ❑ Extended stay
- ❑ OTHER: _____

PACK

TYPE: _____

GEAR

	Used (Y/N)		Used (Y/N)
❑ Compass		❑ Blanket	
❑ Cord		❑ Axe	
❑ Cup		❑ Rope	
❑ Lighter		❑ Water bottle	
❑ Stakes		❑	
❑ Pot		❑	
❑ Tarp		❑	
❑ Knife		❑	
❑ Skillet		❑	

 **CAMPSITE**

SHELTER

- ❏ Tent
- ❏ Hammock and tarp
- ❏ Fly
- ❏ A-frame
- ❏ Lean-to
- ❏ Wedge
- ❏ OTHER: _____
- ❏ OTHER: _____

OBSERVATIONS

WILDLIFE:
_____
_____
_____

TREES AND OTHER FLORA:
_____
_____
_____

RIVERS, LAKES, OTHER WATER:
_____
_____
_____

CAMPSITE ACTIVITY

BUILDS:
_____
_____
_____

TRAPPED:
_____
_____
_____

HUNTED/FISHED:
_____
_____
_____

GENERAL FIELD NOTES

GENERAL FIELD NOTES

GENERAL FIELD NOTES

LOCATION:

DATE:

COORDINATES: _____ ELEVATION: _____

TERRAIN: _____

WEATHER:

TEMPERATURE: _____ CONDITIONS: _____

DURATION

- ❑ Loop
- ❑ Out and back
- ❑ Day trip
- ❑ Overnight
- ❑ Extended stay
- ❑ OTHER: _____

PACK

TYPE: _____

GEAR

	Used (Y/N)		Used (Y/N)
❑ Compass		❑ Blanket	
❑ Cord		❑ Axe	
❑ Cup		❑ Rope	
❑ Lighter		❑ Water bottle	
❑ Stakes		❑	
❑ Pot		❑	
❑ Tarp		❑	
❑ Knife		❑	
❑ Skillet		❑	

CAMPSITE

SHELTER
- ❏ Tent
- ❏ Hammock and tarp
- ❏ Fly
- ❏ A-frame
- ❏ Lean-to
- ❏ Wedge
- ❏ OTHER: _____
- ❏ OTHER: _____

👁 OBSERVATIONS

WILDLIFE:
_____
_____
_____

TREES AND OTHER FLORA:
_____
_____
_____

RIVERS, LAKES, OTHER WATER:
_____
_____
_____

🔥 CAMPSITE ACTIVITY

BUILDS:
_____
_____
_____

TRAPPED:
_____
_____
_____

HUNTED/FISHED:
_____
_____
_____

GENERAL FIELD NOTES

GENERAL FIELD NOTES

GENERAL FIELD NOTES

GENERAL FIELD NOTES

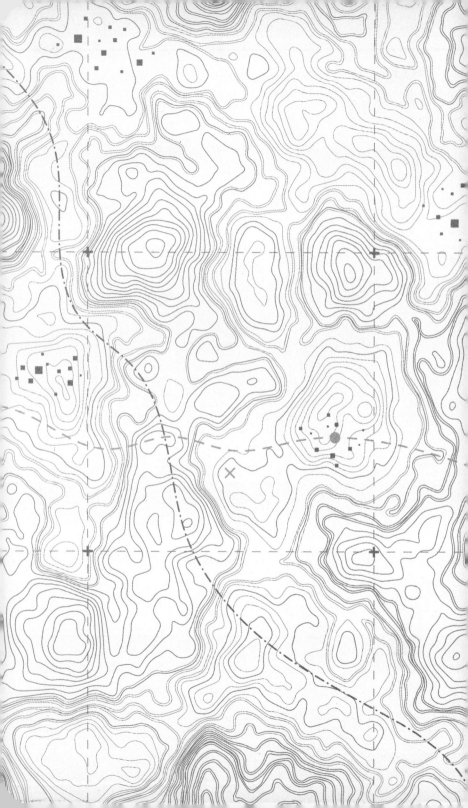